MALCOLM X

MICHAEL BENSON

In Consultation with Martha Cosgrove,
M.A. and Reading Specialist

JUST THE FACTS BIOGRAPHIES

LERNER PUBLICATIONS COMPANY / MINNEAPOLIS

Martha Cosgrove has a master's degree from the University of Minnesota in secondary education, with an emphasis on developmental and remedial reading. She is licensed in 7–12 English and language arts, developmental reading, and remedial reading. She has had several works published, and she gives numerous state and national presentations in her areas of expertise.

Lerner Publications Company
A division of Lerner Publishing Group
241 First Avenue North
Minneapolis, Minnesota U.S.A.

Website address: www.lernerbooks.com

Library of Congress Cataloging-in-Publication Data

Benson, Michael.
   Malcolm X / by Michael Benson.
      p.   cm. – (Just the facts bios)
   Includes bibliographical references and index.
   ISBN: 0-8225-2444-9 (lib. bdg. : alk paper)
   1. X, Malcolm, 1925–1965–Juvenile literature.   2. Black Muslims–Biography–Juvenile literature.   3. African Americans–Biography–Juvenile literature.   I. Title.   II. Series.
BP223.Z8L5719 2005
320.54'6'092–dc22   2004021255

Manufactured in the United States of America
1 2 3 4 5 6 – JR – 10 09 08 07 06 05

CONTENTS

CHAPTER 1

TERROR IN THE NIGHT

MALCOLM X WAS BORN as Malcolm Little in the early 1900s. During this time, black men and women in America were treated as second-class citizens. African Americans, who were politely called Negroes in those days, faced all kinds of obstacles to having the same rights as white people. These obstacles were especially hard to overcome in the southern United States.

In the South, African Americans were not allowed to use "whites-only" drinking fountains, restaurants, or restrooms. They sat in the back of buses, while white people sat in the front. Worst of all, black people in America were not supposed to try to improve their lives. They were supposed to work for little money or starve. And they were supposed to quietly accept this treatment.

4

In the early 1900s, African Americans sat in the back rows of public buses.

Malcolm X didn't accept that idea. He lived most of his life fighting against it. And he didn't fight quietly either.

EARLY YEARS

Malcolm Little was born on May 19, 1925. His parents were Louise and Earl Little. Earl was a minister from the southern state of Georgia. He didn't accept being a second-class citizen. But he also believed that blacks could never make their situation in America better. As a result, he thought African Americans should leave white society and return to Africa. (Many black families had first come to America as slaves or as servants to white families.)

In spite of his beliefs, he still took care of his family by working in America. Earl worked at many different odd jobs to pay his family's bills. He also worked with Marcus Garvey, a well-known African American activist. (An activist works actively for a certain cause.) Like Earl, Garvey believed that African Americans would be better off if they returned to the African continent.

Louise was Earl's second wife. She had been born in Grenada, a Caribbean island nation, of a black mother and a white father. Louise was a well-educated woman, but she found that her education did not do her much good in the United States. She

IT'S A FACT!

In 1918, Earl Little and Louise Langdon Norton met at a meeting for people who supported Marcus Garvey and the back-to-Africa movement.

was still black. And most black women could find work only in jobs that required little training, such as being a maid or a cleaning woman.

Malcolm was the fourth of eight children. The oldest child was Wilfred. Then came Hilda, Philbert, and Malcolm. Malcolm was followed by Reginald, Yvonne, Wesley, and Robert. Malcolm also had an older half brother, also named Earl, and two older half sisters, Ella and Mary. These were Earl's children from his first marriage. These three children lived in the North, in Boston, Massachusetts. Earl, Louise, and their eight children lived in Nebraska, part of the midwestern United States. Even though Nebraska wasn't part of the South, it still wasn't easy for African Americans to succeed there.

Malcolm had the lightest skin of any child in the family. He looked like his mother more than his father. Malcolm's hair and skin were reddish brown, while his brothers and sisters had darker coloring. (At the time, some people thought that a black person with paler skin might be mistaken as white. Looking white could be helpful in getting a job.)

THE HAZARDS OF BEING BLACK

By the time of Malcolm's birth in 1925, it had been sixty years since the end of the Civil War (1861–1865). African Americans were freed from slavery after the war. But even after the war, living conditions for black people had not improved very much. The only jobs black people could get didn't pay much. They usually involved serving or cleaning up after white people. Blacks weren't even able to move around freely. When Malcolm was a little boy, laws in many towns prevented black people from being in the white section of town after dark.

In the southern states, laws kept black and white people apart, or segregated. Public facilities, such as drinking fountains, train and bus stations, restrooms, and theaters, were segregated. These facilities were labeled either "White" or "Colored." Black children could not attend school with white children. Black children were kept out of libraries, parks, and

swimming pools. White children attended schools in nice buildings. Black children went to school in run-down, overcrowded shacks. This system of

An African American man drinks from a segregated water cooler.

forced separation based on race—called segregation—affected almost every part of life in the South. And it remained the law because white people kept black people from voting. Southern lawmakers had created special voting requirements, such as passing a very hard reading test. These requirements made it almost impossible for most African Americans to vote. As a result, the segregation laws stayed in place.

In the northern states, segregation was not required by law, as it was in the South. After the Civil War, many African American families had moved to the North in search of a better life. But even in the North, black people were treated unfairly. They soon learned that good jobs and housing were hard to find if you were black. This unfair treatment in the search for basic human needs, such as jobs and housing, is called racial discrimination.

African Americans who spoke actively against discrimination were called "troublemakers" by some white people and even some black people. These blacks worried that white people would come after the troublemakers. They feared all black people would end up getting hurt.

The danger was real. White racist groups such as the Ku Klux Klan (KKK) terrorized African

The Ku Klux Klan terrorized the Little family and other African American citizens.

American people. Blacks who tried to fight against racial segregation and discrimination were special targets. Klan members and other white mobs killed many blacks. It wasn't safe to be an activist in the South—or even in Nebraska.

Malcolm's father worked for the Universal Negro Improvement Association (UNIA). Marcus Garvey led the group. Its goal was to help African Americans become independent of white people. As long as Earl Little was working with UNIA, he and his family were in danger. One night, a group of Klansmen on horseback rode circles around the Littles' house. They broke every window before riding off. After a number of these threats, the Littles decided to leave Nebraska.

MARCUS GARVEY

Marcus Garvey *(right)* was born in 1887 on the Caribbean island of Jamaica in the West Indies. At the time, this island was a colony of Britain. Garvey traveled around the Caribbean as a young man. He saw the poor living conditions of black people. He also saw how hopeless they felt. Everywhere he went, white people seemed to be mistreating black people.

Over time, Garvey learned of the Pan-African (all-African) movement. This movement encouraged black people around the world to stop depending on white people and to take control of their own lives. Inspired by the idea of black independence, Garvey started the Universal Negro Improvement Association. His goal was to encourage black people everywhere to work together and promote black pride. Garvey brought his idea of black pride to the United States in 1918. During the next seven years, he gained tens of thousands of supporters, including Earl Little.

Garvey was a thinker and a writer as well as a political leader. He believed that black people should look to Africa as their spiritual home, no matter where they actually lived. He encouraged his followers to create black businesses and schools. One of Garvey's projects was the Black Star Line, a shipping company intended to take African Americans back to Africa. Three ships were built before the company ran out of money. Garvey was eventually convicted of mail fraud (using the mail for illegal purposes) and forced to leave the United States. He died in Britain in 1940.

To escape the KKK, the Littles moved farther north. In 1929, by the time Malcolm was four, the family had settled in Lansing, Michigan.

For a while, Malcolm's home life was loving. He was a smart, lively child. He soon learned that he had a better chance of getting his way by making a fuss than he had by being quiet. He was happiest when his father took him to UNIA meetings, where Earl would speak. Malcolm loved watching his father preach.

The family raised chickens and had a big garden. Malcolm tended his own small area of the garden. He was very proud of the peas he grew. "I would pull out the grass in my garden by hand when the first little blades came up," he remembered. "I would patrol the rows on my hands and knees for any worms and bugs, and I would kill and bury them. And sometimes when I had everything straight and clean for my things to grow, I would lie down on my back between two rows, and I would gaze up in the blue sky at the clouds moving and think all kinds of things." This was a peaceful time for young Malcolm.

Even though personal life for the Littles had started to go right, life outside the home began to go very wrong. In 1929, Earl bought a house in a white section of Lansing. White neighbors were angry that an African American family had moved onto the block. They soon claimed that the law said the house had to be sold to white people. The Littles refused to move. In the middle of the night, a white mob surrounded the house. Malcolm's mother came to the door. The mob asked to see Earl, and she told them he was out of town. The mob then set fire to the house, as a way of saying "get out."

Watching his home burn was Malcolm's first clear childhood memory. He was standing in the backyard in the middle of the night. "The white police and firemen came and stood around watching as the house burned down to the ground," he wrote later. Earl built his family a new house in another part of town.

The white racists of Lansing were not done with the Littles, however. In 1931, when Malcolm was six years old, some men came to the house with the news that Earl Little was dead. He had been beaten and laid across the streetcar tracks. He wasn't found until after a streetcar had run over him.

Earl owned a large life insurance policy. (A person who buys life insurance makes regular payments to an insurance company over a period of time. If that person dies by accident or from illness, the insurance company pays a certain amount of money to the family left behind.) Earl had bought insurance to make sure that his family would have money to live on if something happened to him.

But when he died, the money didn't come. Instead, the insurance company said that Earl had bashed in his own head and had dragged himself across the tracks. Company officials said that Earl had committed suicide. And, according to the company's rules, suicides weren't covered by insurance. As a result, the company refused to make any payment to the family.

A SCATTERED FAMILY

At first, Louise was able to land jobs sewing or keeping house for white people. Many white people didn't want African Americans in their houses. But Louise was light-skinned enough to be mistaken for a white woman. When her employers saw Louise's children and realized that she was black, she was fired. Louise was very upset.

She did her best to keep the family together, but soon the stress became too much for her. By about 1935, ten-year-old Malcolm began to notice a difference in his mother. Sometimes she didn't seem to know where she was. She began to talk to herself. At times, she didn't know that Malcolm and his brothers and sisters were in the room with her. She cried all the time.

IT'S A FACT!

Malcolm's older brother Wilfred quit school to find work. He would come home at night exhausted and gave whatever money he made to his mother.

Social welfare workers (people from the government who are charged with taking care of the health and educational needs of children from troubled families) began coming to the house. They asked the children questions. Louise Little became angrier and angrier with the welfare people. She was sure they were trying to break up her family. But in the end, it was Louise's own mental illness that broke up the family. In 1937, Louise was taken to a hospital for patients with mental illness. She could no longer take care of her children, so they became the responsibility of the government. They were split up and sent to foster, or temporary, homes, as if they were orphans. Malcolm lived with a friendly neighborhood family, the Gohannases.

The Little children continued to see each other as often as they could, even though they were living in different houses.

In 1938, Malcolm started seventh grade at West Junior High School. He was the only African American student. Malcolm did well in his classes and was popular with the other students. He was elected class president. Malcolm later said he felt that the white people saw him as a pet, not as a human being. He felt that their acceptance of him wasn't real.

In 1939, while Malcolm was going to junior high school, he met his half sister Ella for the first time. She had come from Boston to visit her sisters and brothers in Michigan. Ella was a respected and educated twenty-four-year-old. She had worked hard and had saved her money. She had also bought property that had increased in value. She had helped other family members move to Boston. Malcolm was very impressed with her.

"She was the first really proud black woman I had ever seen in my life," he wrote. "She was plainly proud of her very dark skin. This was unheard of among Negroes in those days, especially in Lansing. . . . The way she sat, moved, talked, did everything, [showed that she was] somebody who did and got exactly what she wanted."

A turning point in Malcolm's life came later that year. One day at school, Malcolm's English teacher asked him what he wanted to be when he grew up. Malcolm replied that he was thinking of becoming a lawyer. The teacher said, "Malcolm, one of life's first needs is for us to be realistic. Don't misunderstand me, now. We all here like you, you know that. But . . . you need to think of something you can be. . . . Why don't you plan on carpentry?"

Malcolm was deeply hurt when he heard this. There didn't seem to be any point in dreaming. He understood his teacher believed that an African American man could not hope to improve himself in a society controlled by whites. Within a short time, Malcolm wrote to Ella. He told her how much he would like to come to Boston. Ella agreed. She arranged to become Malcolm's adult guardian. In 1940, at age fifteen, Malcolm dropped out of school and headed for Boston to see what he could learn on his own.

2 HUSTLING

FIFTEEN-YEAR-OLD MALCOLM was more than six feet tall and slender. He looked older and more mature than he was. He told Ella that he wanted to get a job. She said fine, but not right away. First, he should get to know the city, especially Roxbury, an African American neighborhood in Boston. Later, she said, she would help him get a job.

Ella hoped that Malcolm would use this period of freedom to meet the leading citizens of Roxbury.

Most of these people lived in an area known as the Hill. But that wasn't what Malcolm did. Instead, he began to hang out at Roxbury's rough bars and pool halls. At one of the pool halls, Malcolm met a man named Shorty Jarvis. Shorty had also come from Lansing. He could see that Malcolm was still a little new to the ways of the streets, so he tried to teach him.

When Ella got Malcolm the job she'd promised, it turned out to be shining shoes at the Roseland Ballroom. The Roseland was a dance hall in Boston. The best bands in the world, both black and white, played at the Roseland. Shorty taught Malcolm some ways to make the white men give him bigger tips.

Shorty told Malcolm to "Tom a little." He wanted Malcolm to act like an Uncle Tom, a quiet black man who behaves like a servant in front of white people. So Malcolm kept his head down and worked hard.

Being a humble shoeshine boy did not fit Malcolm's style, however. He soon learned that he could make a lot more money illegally selling marijuana to Roseland's customers. Whether he was shining shoes or selling drugs, Malcolm got to meet

some of the greatest musicians of his day at
Roseland. These musicians included Count Basie,
Lionel Hampton, and Duke Ellington.

When he went out with his friends, Malcolm
dressed in a sharp-looking zoot suit. Zoot suits had
wide shoulders and baggy pants. He wore a
matching wide-brimmed hat with a feather in it.

Denzel Washington (who played Malcolm in the movie *Malcolm X*) as Malcolm in his zoot suit

Shorty used lye, a harsh chemical, to "conk," or straighten, Malcolm's hair. This was the style at that time. "This was my first really big step toward self-degradation [humiliating myself]," Malcolm later wrote. "I endured all of that pain, literally burning my flesh to have it look like a white man's hair."

IT'S A FACT!

The word *conk* comes from Congolene, a product used to straighten the hair of African Americans. Most people, however, used a homemade mixture of lye and potatoes instead. Real Congolene cost a lot of money.

But Malcolm wasn't thinking about that when he had his hair straightened. He was thinking about dancing. "Malcolm was like a Romeo," remembered Shorty Jarvis. "All the girls were after him." Malcolm liked to dance with the ladies at the ballroom. "I just about went wild. . . . " he said. "I was whirling girls so fast their skirts were snapping."

THE FAST LIFE

Malcolm soon quit his job at the Roseland. He took a better job as a soda fountain clerk in a shop in the nice part of Roxbury. At the shop, he met a girl his age named Laura. She was just the sort of girl Ella wanted Malcolm to meet. Laura was interested in education. She told Malcolm that it wasn't too late for him. If he went back to school, he could become a lawyer, just like he had dreamed.

Laura explained that no matter what Malcolm's teacher in Michigan had said, a black man could become a lawyer in America. It might not be as easy as it would be for a white person, but it could be done. However, Malcolm was too caught up in his street ways to understand what she was saying.

One night, soon after they began dating, Malcolm took Laura to a dance at the Roseland

Ballroom. While they were there, Malcolm met a white woman named Sophia. Later, when he wrote his life story, Malcolm didn't mention Sophia's last name or her age. He did make it clear that she was older, experienced, and wild. Malcolm quickly took Laura home and returned to the Roseland to meet Sophia. According to Malcolm, Laura was so hurt by the experience that her life fell apart.

Malcolm wasn't interested in a serious relationship or concerned with the future. Like many young men his age, he was more interested in the fun he could have right now. This kind of thinking led him more and more into a life of crime.

Malcolm had heard that Harlem was the most fun and exciting place to be. Harlem is a neighborhood in the northern part of New York City, more than 150 miles from Boston. Harlem was the center of black culture. And white people flocked there too. In Harlem, the best music was played and the coolest people hung out. It was also a place that had never completely bounced back after the great economic hardships of the Depression (1929–1939).

Malcolm got his chance to go to Harlem in December 1941. At this same time, Japanese forces bombed Pearl Harbor, a naval base in the

Hawaiian Islands. After this bombing, the United States entered into World War II (1939–1945).

That month, Malcolm landed a job working for the Yankee Clipper train. This train traveled between Boston and New York. Malcolm was a kitchen helper. His job was to wash dishes, take out the garbage, sell sandwiches to passengers, and clean up after the chef.

As soon as Malcolm got a taste of the lively world of Harlem, he knew that this was where he wanted to be. He was only sixteen, but he moved out of his sister's house and into a boardinghouse in Harlem.

DETROIT RED

Away from Ella, Malcolm quickly picked up more bad habits. He continued to sell marijuana, and he also smoked a lot of it himself. He began using cocaine too. The drugs gave him a false sense of control over his life. Because of the cocaine, Malcolm was often pushy and rude at work on the train. The customers complained, and it wasn't long before Malcolm was fired.

His next job was working at a Harlem restaurant called Small's Paradise. This was a hangout for Harlem criminals. Malcolm met people at Small's Paradise with colorful nicknames like West Indian Archie, Sammy the Pimp, Dollarbill, and Fewclothes. Malcolm was given a nickname of his own during this time. Because of his reddish skin and hair and his Michigan childhood, he became known as Detroit Red, after Michigan's largest city.

While he worked as a waiter, Malcolm made extra money as a "steerer." If someone came to

Malcolm worked at Small's Paradise (above) after he was fired from his train job.

Harlem looking for drugs or prostitutes, Malcolm's job was to steer the person to the right place. The people he steered were usually white men. "He was a beautiful con man," Shorty Jarvis said of his friend. "He was a thinker."

Malcolm's crimes kept getting worse. Soon he and his buddies were committing robberies with guns. But Malcolm didn't feel guilty about his crimes. He believed that an African American man didn't stand a chance of making an honest living in a society controlled by whites. His only option was "hustling," as people on the streets called the criminal activity. "Everybody in Harlem needed some kind of hustle to survive," he said. One day, Malcolm steered a man to a prostitute. It turned out the man worked for the police. A detective came to Small's and took Malcolm to a police station. He wasn't arrested, but he did lose his job.

Malcolm was living a dangerous life. He almost lost his life several times during these months. He never went anywhere without carrying several handguns. If an argument broke out with another hustler, neither side was going to back down. The guns often came out. At least once, Malcolm was roughed up by Harlem gangsters.

They thought he had ripped them off in a drug deal. Life on the streets was becoming more and more dangerous, but Malcolm did nothing to change his actions. He saw no other way to live.

After losing his job at Small's, Malcolm didn't get another honest job. Instead, he took the advice of Sammy the Pimp. Malcolm became a full-time criminal.

HARD TIMES IN HARLEM

Malcolm turned eighteen in May 1943. World War II was still raging, and Malcolm was ordered to appear before the draft board. (A draft board selects, or drafts, young men for military service.) But Malcolm had no intention of being drafted into the army. He didn't want to fight in what he viewed as a white man's war. He came up with a plan. He decided he would act crazy during his army physical examination, hoping the army would disqualify him.

According to Malcolm's version of the story, he wore his most outrageous zoot suit to the draft interview. He told the doctors that he couldn't wait to get a gun and start shooting white folks. That did it. Malcolm was rated 4-F. This rating made it impossible for the military to take him.

CIVIL RIGHTS AND WORLD WAR II

African Americans had been fighting for equal rights as U.S. citizens since the end of the Civil War. Demands for equal rights reached a new peak during World War II. More than one million black soldiers had joined the fight to end the racist leadership in Germany. But, at the same time, these black soldiers knew they were still being treated as second-class citizens back home. Blacks also protested the army's policy of segregation.

In 1942, a religion student named James Farmer started the Congress of Racial Equality (CORE). Farmer wanted to fight segregation using nonviolent methods. CORE pioneered two forms of nonviolent protest. One was the sit-in, in which black people refused to leave a "whites-only" place by simply sitting down. The other was the freedom ride, in which black people fought against the segregation on buses by breaking the rules on purpose.

The National Association for the Advancement of Colored People (NAACP) also fought for equal rights. In the 1940s, NAACP lawyers began to argue against segregation before the judges of the U.S. Supreme Court. Because of these arguments, the Court made a decision that said separate schools for blacks and whites goes against the U.S. Constitution. Segregation became illegal. This development set the stage for the civil rights movement of the 1950s and 1960s.

At the time, racial tensions in Harlem were heating up. A young Harlem politician named Adam Clayton Powell Jr. was leading protests against the lack of jobs and housing for black people. These protests made African Americans more aware of the problems.

One night in August 1943, the anger that had been building up in Harlem finally exploded. A white police officer killed a black soldier in a Harlem hotel. Riots broke out. Five people were killed, and more than four hundred were injured.

The riots also killed what was left of the Harlem economy. Because of the racial tension, white people stopped going to Harlem to spend their money. The community became poorer than ever.

For a time, Malcolm made money running an illegal lottery (money pool) in Harlem. Things got

A mounted police officer patrols a Harlem street after the night of riots on August 2, 1943.

even worse for Malcolm when he was accused of cheating in a card game. West Indian Archie swore that he would kill Malcolm. Word got out that Malcolm was in big trouble. The news even made it up to Boston.

One night in 1945, Malcolm was walking down the street. He was trying to avoid being noticed. Suddenly, a car pulled up to the curb. It was Malcolm's old friend Shorty Jarvis. Shorty told Malcolm to get in, and he took him to Boston. This act probably saved Malcolm's life.

3 CHANGE IN PRISON

MALCOLM HAD MADE a lot of money in New York. But when he arrived in Boston in 1945, he was broke. Most of his money had gone to pay for his drug habit. Malcolm was spending twenty dollars a day (now about two hundred dollars) for cocaine and five dollars (now about fifty dollars) for marijuana.

In Boston, Malcolm set up a house burglary business along with Shorty and Shorty's girlfriend. Sophia, whom Malcolm had continued to see over the years, was also involved.

Sophia and Shorty's girlfriend were both white. They were sent out in advance to see if anyone was home in the targeted houses. They would come back and tell the men. Malcolm and Shorty would then rob the unoccupied homes. They sold the stolen goods to pawnshops.

In one house, Malcolm stole a watch that needed repair. The owner of the watch reported that it had been stolen. He also told the police that it was broken. When Malcolm took the watch to a repair shop, the police were watching the place. Malcolm was arrested. He and Shorty were convicted of burglary, and Malcolm was sentenced

A police picture of Malcolm after his arrest in 1945

to ten years in prison. That was more time than most burglars got for a first offense.

Malcolm and Shorty entered Charlestown State Prison in Boston in February 1946. Malcolm was twenty years old. Shorty described their prison life this way: "The cell was six by twelve feet. You got a hard cot, a bucket of water, and a bucket [to use as a toilet]. No running water. Unsanitary. Filthy!"

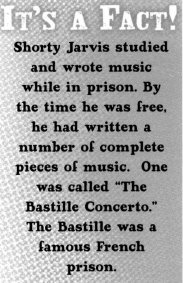

IT'S A FACT!

Shorty Jarvis studied and wrote music while in prison. By the time he was free, he had written a number of complete pieces of music. One was called "The Bastille Concerto." The Bastille was a famous French prison.

THE BLACK MUSLIMS

While he was in prison, Malcolm learned about the Nation of Islam. This is an African American religious group that was headed by a man named Elijah Muhammad. The group's beliefs were based on the ancient world religion of Islam, whose followers are called Muslims. Like other Muslims, the members of the Nation of Islam worship Allah (God).

ELIJAH MUHAMMAD

The original name of Elijah Muhammad *(below)* was Elijah Poole. He was born around October 7, 1897, in a rural part of Georgia. Elijah was one of twelve children born to William and Marie Poole. His father was a minister.

In 1919, Elijah married Clara Evans, with whom he had eight children. At the time of his marriage, Elijah worked for the railroad and for a brick company. But in April 1923, he took his family northward to Detroit, Michigan. There he got a job working on an automobile assembly line.

In 1930, Elijah met Wallace D. Fard, the founder of the Nation of Islam. Wallace Fard preached that it was time for black people to return to Islam, which he viewed as the religion of their ancient ancestors. When Elijah met him, Fard was selling silk products door-to-door. However, he said he was a prophet who came from Africa to help African Americans understand their history and their place in the world. According to Fard, the black race was the superior "original race." And black Americans were Islam's lost sheep. His job was to herd the sheep and bring them back home.

Elijah became Fard's main assistant and devoted follower. Fard gave

Elijah the Muslim name Muhammad. (Muhammad is the prophet of the ancient religion of Islam.) Fard disappeared on February 26, 1934. To this day, no one knows what happened to him. After his disappearance, Elijah took control of the Nation of Islam.

In the 1940s, the Nation of Islam tried to increase its membership. Members preached the message of black power to people in poor areas and prisons. This is when Malcolm joined the group.

Members of the Nation of Islam were sometimes known as Black Muslims. The religion set forth two strong beliefs. One was the view that white people were the source of all evil. The other view was that blacks were Allah's chosen people who would someday rise above the white devils.

These statements may seem extreme. But to Malcolm they made a lot of sense. After all, he knew white people had killed his father. He had watched his mother's mental collapse afterward. The teachings of Elijah Muhammad also reminded Malcolm of the ideas of his father and Marcus Garvey. In some ways, Malcolm probably saw Elijah as a father figure. Elijah and Earl Little had been born only seventy miles apart in rural Georgia. Both men had similar ideas and goals, such as black pride and brotherhood. And, like Earl Little, Elijah had gone northward to Michigan hoping to find more freedom and opportunity.

Malcolm did not know that the teachings of the Nation of Islam are very different from those of traditional Islam. The Islamic religion is practiced in the Middle East and elsewhere around the world. Traditional Islam teaches that all people are brothers and sisters, regardless of race. However,

Elijah Muhammad *(center, behind podium)* speaks at a Nation of Islam meeting in Chicago, Illinois.

the Nation of Islam taught that the black race was God's favorite and that white people were evil devils. Members of the Nation of Islam worshiped Elijah Muhammad as a prophet. Traditional Muslims do not share these views at all.

In 1948, Malcolm was moved to Norfolk Prison Colony. Norfolk is also in Massachusetts. This prison was nicer than the first one. At least it had toilets that flushed. In late 1949, Malcolm began to write to Elijah Muhammad. He declared himself to be a Muslim. Malcolm adopted the ways of the Black Muslims, who believe in having a clean body, a clean mind, and a clean spirit. Members do not drink, smoke, or eat pork. They also do not believe in sex outside of marriage.

WORD POWER

Malcolm wanted to educate himself and to improve his writing skills. He copied one page from the dictionary into a notebook each day. The prison had a very large library. He also read the encyclopedia and many other books. Malcolm read the Bible and *Outline of History* by author H. G. Wells. He read books about genetics (the passing of human traits from generation to generation) and the classic antislavery novel *Uncle Tom's Cabin,* written in 1852.

"LIGHTS OUT"

The prison had a 10:00 P.M. "lights out" rule. But Malcolm continued to read until the early morning hours. He studied philosophy, science, and religion. He used the light that came into his cell from the hallway. When a guard passed, Malcolm moved to his bunk and pretended to be asleep. Later on, he blamed these long hours of reading in low light for his need to wear glasses.

When Malcolm started his self-improvement program, he knew and could use only a few hundred words. His handwriting was so poor that he could not write in a straight line. But by 1950, after four years in prison, he had greatly increased his knowledge of the English language, world events, and history.

With his new language skills, Malcolm began a letter-writing campaign on behalf of the Nation of Islam. He wrote daily letters to his brothers Philbert and Reginald, to his sister Hilda, and to Elijah Muhammad. He also wrote to government officials demanding an end to racial injustice. He sent letters to many of his old criminal friends. He told them that he had changed his ways, and he invited them to join the Nation of Islam.

In prison, Malcolm organized discussion groups for men interested in learning about being Black Muslims. He told stories about past African civilizations. He also spoke about the poor treatment of African

IT'S A FACT!

Malcolm X later said that he blocked out a lot of memories from prison, but that he never lost his memory of the bars in his cell.

Americans by whites in modern times. Prisoners who knew him when he first arrived in prison were amazed at the change in Malcolm. Before his religious change, he was an angry young man whom the other prisoners called Satan. Although he was still angry, Malcolm had become very focused. He hoped to use his anger to improve the world.

4

MINISTER

(Above) After his release from prison, Malcolm wore closely cut hair and neat suits.

MALCOLM WAS RELEASED from prison on parole in August 1952. (Under the parole system, a prisoner can be released early so long as the prisoner stays out of trouble and stays in touch with a parole officer.) A free man, Malcolm immediately went to Detroit to live with his brother Wilfred. Wilfred managed a furniture store. He gave Malcolm a job there as a salesperson.

Malcolm no longer wore his hair straightened. Instead, he kept it natural and cut very short. This is the style of Black Muslim men. They looked sharp in their black suits, white shirts, and slender black ties. Malcolm replaced his prison eyeglasses with a better-looking pair.

Malcolm attended meetings at a Nation of Islam temple in Detroit. Wilfred and his family also attended these meetings. (In the Islamic religion, worship takes place in a temple or mosque.) Because of his good speaking skills, Malcolm was given the job of recruiting, or bringing in, new members. He also continued to read many books and to study the teachings of Elijah Muhammad.

IT'S A FACT!

Malcolm's sister Hilda thought moving to Detroit would be a good idea because Malcolm could join a temple there with other practicing Muslims. Ella said it was a good idea because the police in a new city wouldn't be watching for Malcolm like they would in New York or Boston.

MEETING ELIJAH

Malcolm finally got to meet Elijah Muhammad in person. The meeting took place in Detroit in September 1952. Malcolm hadn't been so excited about anything since he was a child. During the meeting, Elijah Muhammad congratulated Malcolm for being so strong and for following the Muslim traditions while he was in prison.

But Elijah told Malcolm that it was easy to be good in prison. The outside world had more temptation to do wrong. Malcolm still had to prove himself outside of prison. But Elijah was sure that Malcolm was going to remain a faithful Black Muslim as a free man. Malcolm openly worshiped Elijah. "I had more faith in Elijah Muhammad than I could ever have in any other man upon this earth," he said.

The Nation of Islam believed that a black man's last name was meaningless. In the 1700s and 1800s, black people in the United States usually didn't have last names. The names of their ancestors in Africa had usually been forgotten or ignored. When slaves became free, they often took the name of their former white slave owners. This way, family members—who all had the same last name but who had been separated by slavery— would have an easier time finding one another.

The Nation of Islam encouraged its members to stop using these old slave names. In place of that name, members at first used an X. This X

NATION NAMES

When someone wanted to join the Nation of Islam, he or she had to apply to Elijah Muhammad. When the application was approved, the new member received his or her "X." The X was then used as a last name until Elijah later gave the member a new, Islamic name. To avoid having several members with the same name, the Xs were numbered. For example, the first man named John who received his X from Elijah Muhammad became John X. The second man named John was John 2X and so on.

stood for their unknown original African name. Eventually, the members received Islamic last names. For Malcolm, taking the name X was the final step in becoming a new person. It separated him from the person he had been before he began following the teachings of Elijah Muhammad. From this point onward, Malcolm Little became Malcolm X.

SPREADING THE WORD

Malcolm X was very good at recruiting new members into the Nation of Islam. His success helped move him into a new role. In the summer of 1953, Malcolm was named assistant minister at the temple in Detroit.

During this time, the Korean War (1950–1953) was being fought. The conflict had begun in June 1950 between Communist North Korea and non-Communist South Korea. The United States became involved on the side of South Korea. And once again, Malcolm was called before the draft board. This time, he did not act crazy to keep himself out of military

In the 1950s, the Nation of Islam had great success attracting new members. Here a large crowd gathers at a rally in Chicago, Illinois.

service. Instead, he refused to serve because of his religious beliefs. He became a conscientious objector. A conscientious objector believes that war is morally wrong and therefore can't participate in one. Malcolm's position was respected, and the military let him avoid service.

In early 1954, Elijah sent Malcolm to Boston to start a new temple. Malcolm's sister Ella still lived there. The changes in Malcolm surprised his old friends in Boston. On the other hand, Malcolm was upset to see that his friends had not changed much at all. They had just gone farther down a bad road. They still lived a life of crime, and they were still addicted to drugs.

When the Boston temple was set up and running smoothly, Elijah moved Malcolm to Philadelphia, Pennsylvania. He spent three months setting up another temple there.

Malcolm's work was very successful. In the summer of 1954, Elijah promoted Malcolm once again. In fact, Malcolm was given a dream job as minister of the temple in Harlem. Malcolm gave great speeches. Each week, more new faces appeared in the temple to hear Malcolm's fiery talks. He preached the beliefs of Elijah Muhammad.

But his preaching also carried the excitement and energy of both Earl Little and of Marcus Garvey, the leader who had inspired Earl.

SISTER BETTY

In 1956, someone new joined the Harlem temple. Malcolm called her Sister Betty X. (Members of the Nation of Islam called one another "brother" and "sister," even though the members weren't related.)

She had a fine mind and a strong spirit. She had been born in Detroit as Betty Sanders. She had studied at the Tuskegee Institute, the Brooklyn State Hospital School of Nursing, and Jersey City State College. Malcolm sensed that Sister Betty could be a good wife for him.

Malcolm arranged for Betty to meet Elijah Muhammad. Elijah agreed that she was a fine woman. Malcolm took his time, but eventually he asked Betty to marry him. She said yes. Betty and Malcolm were married on January 14, 1958, by a justice of the peace in Lansing, Michigan.

Soon after the wedding, Malcolm's sister Ella finally became part of the Nation of Islam. She had gone to meetings for years, but she had refused to join. Malcolm thought she would never leave the Christian church. Her faith in Christianity had seemed so strong. Another exciting event for the family came in 1958. Malcolm and Betty's first child was born. They named their new daughter Attallah.

It's a Fact!

Attallah was named after Attila the Hun. This powerful leader of the Huns (a people of central Asia) challenged the rulers of the ancient Roman Empire.

Fighting Back

People in Harlem had already noticed the Nation of Islam. But the Black Muslims earned real respect in the community because of something that happened in April 1958. The event began with the arrest and beating of a black man named Johnson Hinton. Hinton had seen the police beating another black man, and he had complained. Because he had spoken out, the police turned on Hinton. They beat him and dragged him, bleeding, to jail. He was treated as if he had actually committed a crime.

When news of the beatings reached Malcolm, he called temple members together. They marched

like an army to the police station where Hinton
was being held. Malcolm entered the police station
and demanded to see the prisoner. The other
temple members stood at attention outside.
Malcolm explained that these men would remain
there until his demands were met.

In the meantime, a crowd was gathering
outside the police station. The people wanted to see
what all the fuss was about. Finally, Hinton was
brought to Malcolm. Malcolm demanded that
Hinton be allowed to see a doctor, and he was
taken to the hospital. Only then did Malcolm tell
his "soldiers" to leave.·

Malcolm had stood up to the New York Police
Department, and the police officers had backed
down. By the next day, everyone in Harlem knew
about it. New recruits joined the Nation of Islam
faster than ever before. As much as possible,
temple members were encouraged to live outside
the white man's economic system. They started
their own businesses and worked with other African
American-owned companies.

The Nation's message was very different
from the goals and ideas of the growing civil
rights movement. That movement was guided by

Members of the Nation of Islam temple in New York march to a police station. They were protesting the beating and arrest of Johnson Hinton.

Christian ideas and was led by Martin Luther King Jr., a Christian minister. The civil rights movement used nonviolent methods to bring together, or integrate, blacks and whites in the same schools and other facilities. In every case, angry southern whites resisted the changes.

Malcolm didn't respect the efforts of the civil rights movement. He continued to call for African Americans to create their own separate society. Blacks could not afford to wait patiently for racial justice, he said. Malcolm was against the goal of integration. "It is not integration that Negroes in America want, it is human dignity," he said. If Malcolm made one message clear, it was that African Americans were in charge of their own destiny.

In 1957, in his first national speech, Dr. Martin Luther King Jr. addresses a huge crowd in Washington, D.C.

MARTIN LUTHER KING JR.

Martin Luther King Jr. was born on January 15, 1929, in Atlanta, Georgia. He was the son of a minister. Martin was very smart. He was able to enter Morehouse College in Atlanta at the age of fifteen. He became a minister at the age of nineteen. By the time he was twenty-six years old, he had earned an advanced college degree called a doctorate. This degree allowed people to call him Dr. King.

During the late 1950s and early 1960s, Dr. King became an important figure in the civil rights movement. This movement was a fight against segregation and discrimination.

Dr. King was one of the great speakers of all time. He gave his most famous speech in 1963 in Washington, D.C. Hundreds of thousands of people of all colors had marched to the nation's capital. His speech became known as the "I have a dream" speech. He was named *Time* magazine's "Man of the Year" for 1963. The next year, he was awarded the Nobel Prize for Peace. Dr. King was assassinated on April 4, 1968, in Memphis, Tennessee.

In 1959, at the age of thirty-four, Malcolm began writing a column for the *Amsterdam News.* This was Harlem's community newspaper. Then Elijah Muhammad took over that column. Malcolm wrote for the *Los Angeles Herald Dispatch,* a weekly newspaper for African American readers in California.

MALCOLM AND MARTIN

Martin Luther King Jr. and Malcolm X are often lumped together in history books. However, their ideas and their followers were very different. Dr. King organized freedom rides and protest marches to abolish segregation. He favored the integration of whites and blacks in the United States. On the other hand, Malcolm X and the Nation of Islam believed that the races should live separately. They saw white people as devils. Malcolm sometimes supported boycotts and other forms of protest. But mostly he continued to ignore the gains made by the civil rights movement.

Martin Luther King Jr.'s beliefs were different from Malcolm X's in another very important way. Dr. King believed in using nonviolent methods. Malcolm, however, believed that if a white man attacked an African American man, the black man had the right to defend himself "by any means necessary." Malcolm and Martin met only once. It was a friendly meeting, but they did not come closer to agreeing with one another.

Malcolm shakes hands with Martin Luther King Jr. (left).

The Nation's ideas and events were being written about in big-city newspapers. But Malcolm thought it would be better if the Nation of Islam had its own newspaper. So he formed *Muhammad Speaks*. This national newspaper printed news stories and opinions from the Nation of Islam's point of view. But the Nation was still not growing quickly enough to satisfy Malcolm. New members were coming in dribbles. Malcolm wanted them to come in a flood.

5

GOING PUBLIC

(Above)
Malcolm X
speaks at a
rally in
Washington,
D.C.

THE FLOOD OF ATTENTION that Malcolm hoped for came in late 1959, when CBS television broadcast a program about the Nation of Islam. The show was called "The Hate That Hate Produced." An African American journalist named Louis Lomax made the program, which Elijah Muhammad had approved.

The show gave many people of all colors their first look at the charming young man

54

with the unusual name of Malcolm X. The show
included scenes filmed in Nation of Islam temples
in Washington, D.C.; Chicago; and New York.
Ministers, including Malcolm, were shown
preaching about the brainwashing of black people
by the white devils. The show noted the Nation of
Islam's economic independence from white people.
Black Muslims would only deal with white-owned
companies when it was absolutely necessary.

The show caused an uproar among both whites
and blacks. Many people felt that the Nation of
Islam encouraged violence. Malcolm had never
believed in quietly accepting unfair treatment.
Instead, he believed that black people had the right
to defend themselves if they were attacked by whites.

The television program had another effect too.
It brought in lots of new members. The Nation of
Islam started holding national conventions, and
Elijah Muhammad filled large meeting rooms with
his followers.

Malcolm X became an instant star. In fact, he
became a superstar. "The Hate That Hate
Produced" showed off his powerful speaking style.
Malcolm spoke plainly and directly, using language
that was simple and easy to understand. He seemed

to know what people were thinking and how they felt. He knew their strengths and weaknesses. "Our forefathers weren't the pilgrims," Malcolm would say. "We didn't land on Plymouth Rock. The Rock was landed on us."

After the show, Malcolm's phone was ringing off the hook with requests for interviews. But at the same time, the Federal Bureau of Investigation (FBI) feared that the Nation of Islam was planning violence. It tapped Malcolm's phone so FBI agents could listen in on his conversations. Malcolm suspected that his phone was tapped, but he couldn't prove it.

In September 1960, Malcolm gave the FBI even more to worry about. He met with the Cuban revolutionary leader Fidel Castro. Castro had overthrown the capitalist government in Cuba, which he made into a Communist nation. (In a Communist system, the government controls the economy. In the capitalist United States, the economy is based on privately owned businesses.)

IT'S A FACT!

When Castro visited New York in 1960, the city's leaders prepared a hotel for him downtown. But Castro said he would rather stay in Harlem. He wanted to meet Malcolm X.

Elijah Muhammad *(right)* introduces Malcolm X at a Chicago rally.

In this way, Castro became an enemy of the capitalist United States, but he was still free to visit.

After the meeting, Malcolm made it clear that the Nation of Islam could never be Cuba's ally, or partner. Cuba was Communist, and Communists do not publicly worship any God. But the FBI put Malcolm on its list of possible Communists anyway. Undercover FBI employees began to join the Nation of Islam to spy on him.

Over the next five years, the FBI became more and more sure that Malcolm was a

Communist. It was true that he did blame capitalism for the poor treatment that African Americans received. In a magazine interview, Malcolm said that capitalism needed "blood to suck" in order to succeed. According to Malcolm, that blood came from the most helpless people in society. However, as these helpless people gained power, capitalism would become weaker and weaker. "It's only a matter of time in my opinion before [capitalism] will collapse completely," Malcolm said.

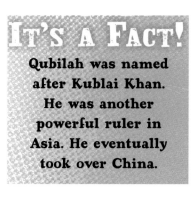

IT'S A FACT!

Qubilah was named after Kublai Khan. He was another powerful ruler in Asia. He eventually took over China.

In December 1960, Malcolm and Betty's second daughter was born. They named her Qubilah. But Malcolm was spending more and more time working and less and less time with his family.

MALCOLM'S MESSAGE

Malcolm's public statements became bolder, and his power grew. But at the same time, the leader of the Nation of Islam was growing weaker. Elijah Muhammad was not a young man, and he suffered from asthma. (Asthma is a disease that affects a person's ability to breathe.) Sometimes Elijah's followers were afraid that he would not make it through a speech because he was coughing so much.

Eventually, Elijah's poor health forced him to retire part-time. He moved to Arizona. The desert air there was good for his lungs. With Elijah gone, Malcolm's role as national spokesperson for the Nation of Islam became more important than ever. But Elijah's son, Wallace D. Muhammad, was

Malcolm X was very comfortable in front of the microphone. He soon became the star of the Nation of Islam.

jealous. So were other top members of the Nation of Islam. They were afraid that Malcolm would take over the organization after Elijah was gone. These people kept Malcolm away from Elijah as much as possible. They told Elijah lies about Malcolm. They wanted Elijah to lose trust in his most successful minister.

But Malcolm was not just successful. He seemed to become the Nation of Islam itself. His speeches continued to bring in new members, especially young African American men and women from the poor areas of major cities. They agreed with Malcolm that the nonviolent protests of the civil rights movement were not producing results fast enough.

Malcolm told his audiences that, for the first time in four hundred years, blacks were learning the real truth. They were learning that white people had brainwashed black people and had stolen their history and self-confidence. Malcolm taught that white people were evil because they kept black people from becoming powerful and successful.

Malcolm's stand against whites offended many African Americans. When a plane crashed in Atlanta and 120 white people were killed, Malcolm called the event "the good news."

After hearing Malcolm preach that white people were evil, someone asked if Malcolm hated white people. Malcolm replied, "What I want to know is how the white man, with the blood of black people dripping off his fingers, can have the [boldness] to be asking black people do they hate him. That takes a lot of nerve."

In 1963, *Playboy* magazine published an interview with Malcolm by Alex Haley. After the interview, Malcolm and Haley continued to work together. They began work on Malcolm's autobiography, his life story.

In the magazine interview, Haley asked Malcolm what the Black Muslims' main goal was. Malcolm replied, "Freedom, justice and equality are our principal ambitions. . . . [a]nd to faithfully serve and follow

IT'S A FACT!

Alex Haley was an African American writer who later published the best-selling book *Roots*. The book explores Haley's journey to find out about his long-ago family in Africa. His family members had been taken away from Africa as slaves. *Roots* was made into a major television miniseries in the 1970s.

Alex Haley with his best-selling book *Roots*

the Honorable Elijah Muhammad.... Mr.
Muhammad... cleans us up—morally, mentally
and spiritually—and he reforms us of the vices
[sins] that have blinded us.... He stops black
men from getting drunk, stops their dope
addiction if they had it, stops nicotine, gambling,
stealing, lying, cheating, fornication [sex outside
of marriage], adultery, prostitution, juvenile
delinquency. I think of this whenever somebody

talks about someone investigating us. Why investigate the Honorable Elijah Muhammad? They should subsidize [financially support] him. He's cleaning up the mess that white men have made."

Malcolm was completely devoted to Elijah Muhammad. He never stopped to think that Elijah might have flaws. He saw Elijah as somewhat less than God, but greater than just a man. But Malcolm learned that Elijah Muhammad didn't always practice what he preached. Men in the Nation of Islam were not allowed to have sexual relations outside of marriage. But Elijah had fathered four children outside his marriage.

It's a Fact!

In 1962, Malcolm and Betty had a third daughter. They named her Ilyasah. Ilyas means Elijah in Arabic. This is the historic language of Islam.

This news shook up everything Malcolm had believed in. He went to Elijah to ask if the stories were true. The leader admitted that they were. But Elijah hoped his weaknesses would not cause people to forget his good deeds.

Malcolm did not feel sorry for Elijah. He was troubled that Elijah did not face up to his weaknesses and admit his wrongs. Malcolm believed that Elijah's followers would have understood that he was only human. Instead, Elijah tried to hide what he had done. Malcolm began to lose his faith in the leader.

TENSION MOUNTS

By the early 1960s, spies populated the Nation of Islam. These men may have been working for white people. Or they may have worked for an African American group that disagreed with the Nation of Islam's ideas. Malcolm did not know for sure. But one thing was clear. The press was reporting on things that Malcolm thought were secret or private. Someone at meetings of the Nation was leaking information to a white reporter.

After that, Malcolm could never be sure that what he was saying was private. And he wasn't sure he could trust what he heard. False rumors were everywhere.

Years later, the truth became known. New information has shown that the New York police and FBI agents had paid men to join the Black

In early 1963, President Kennedy (fifth from right) met with important civil rights leaders at the White House.

Muslims and to report on what happened in meetings. Malcolm found it harder to keep a secret from the FBI. They always seemed to know where he was and what he was doing.

Tensions between Malcolm and Elijah grew. Then a national tragedy made those tensions even worse. On Friday, November 22, 1963, President John F. Kennedy was assassinated in Dallas, Texas. Because of his active support for civil rights laws, Kennedy was one of the most popular U.S. presidents among African Americans.

The death of the president was one of the saddest moments in U.S. history. The African American community was especially worried during the moments following the assassination. They prayed that a black man had not committed the crime. People feared that if a black man were accused of assassinating the president, racial violence would surely break out. When a white man was arrested for the crime, the black community relaxed.

Elijah Muhammad ordered his ministers to keep quiet about the death of the president. But keeping his mouth shut had never been Malcolm's style. On December 1, Malcolm was speaking in New York City. During the question and answer period, he was asked to comment on President Kennedy's assassination. Malcolm ignored Elijah Muhammad's orders. He spoke out, saying he thought it was a case of "the chickens coming home to roost."

IT'S A FACT!

Malcolm believed Elijah used his statement about Kennedy as an excuse to take away Malcolm's power. When he realized this, Malcolm "felt as though something in nature had failed, like the sun, or the stars."

Malcolm later claimed that he was making a general comment. He said he meant that white people, by supporting or allowing violence against black people, were bound to bring violence upon themselves. But the press made it seem as if Malcolm was pleased that the president had been murdered.

Malcolm's words had created a problem for the Nation of Islam. He had also gone against a direct order from Elijah Muhammad. Malcolm was ordered to stay silent in public for ninety days as punishment.

During his forced silence, Malcolm heard rumors that he would not be forgiven for his mistake, even after his punishment was over. The gossip said that Malcolm had betrayed and embarrassed Elijah. According to the rumors, Malcolm would have to die for his mistake.

By this time, everything Malcolm did made the news, even if he didn't want the publicity. For example, reporters wrote about his friendship with the boxer Cassius Clay. The two men had become friends after Clay and his brother attended a Nation of Islam meeting in Detroit.

On February 25, 1964, Clay fought Sonny Liston for the World Heavyweight Boxing

Championship in Miami Beach, Florida. Before the fight, Malcolm and Clay prayed together, and Clay went on to win boxing's greatest prize. Afterward, he announced that he was a member of the Nation of Islam. He also changed his name to Muhammad Ali.

MUHAMMAD ALI

On February 25, 1964, Cassius Clay defeated World Heavyweight Boxing Champion Sonny Liston in seven rounds. This win made Clay the World Heavyweight Champion. But some boxing experts said the event would never happen. Two days before the fight, Bill McDonald, who put up the money for the fight, found out that Clay was a Black Muslim. McDonald said he would call off the fight if Clay didn't leave the Nation of Islam. Clay refused.

The incident upset the public, and Clay received many death threats. He was very worried. Before the fight, Malcolm X went to Clay's dressing room, and they prayed together. Clay decided that, during the fight, only Muslims could give him drinking water and could wipe the sweat from his face. Even his longtime trainer, Angelo Dundee, was not allowed to touch Clay's face between rounds. After the victory, Clay told the world that he'd joined the Nation of Islam.

Malcolm X poses with Muhammad Ali as he signs autographs in New York City.

CHAPTER

6 TRUE ISLAM

(Above)
Malcolm X
announces
that he is
leaving the
Nation of
Islam.

THE PROBLEMS AND RUMORS

surrounding Malcolm needed to end. He called
a press conference in March 1964 to announce
that he was leaving the Nation of Islam. When
he had joined the organization in the late
1940s, it had had four hundred members.
When he left, there were forty thousand.

Malcolm's split from Elijah Muhammad
made front-page news across the country.
Members of the Nation of Islam felt betrayed.
Some Black Muslims publicly criticized
Malcolm. One of them was Louis Farrakhan,

69

whom Malcolm had recruited nine years earlier. Since then, Farrakhan had risen to an important position as leader of the Nation's Boston temple.

LOUIS FARRAKHAN

Louis Farrakhan, the spokesperson for the Nation of Islam, was born on May 11, 1933, in Roxbury, Massachusetts. His birth name was Louis Eugene Walcott. He was raised by his mother, a native of Saint Kitts, an island in the West Indies. At an early age, Louis and his brother Alvin learned the value of education, work, and responsibility. Their mother also taught them about the African American struggle for equality, freedom, and justice.

Louis had a talent for music. So his mother gave him a violin for his sixth birthday. By the age of age thirteen, he was so good that he had played with the Boston College Orchestra and the Boston Civic Symphony. Louis graduated from high school at the age of sixteen. Because he was also a track-and-field star, he earned a scholarship to Winston-Salem Teachers College in North Carolina.

Louis married his childhood sweetheart in September 1953. He was then in his senior year of college. Because he needed money to support his new family, Louis quit college and became a professional performing artist. He sang, danced, and played the violin to make a living. While performing in 1955, Louis was invited to visit one of the Nation of Islam's temples. Soon afterward, he joined the organization and became known as Louis X.

Louis gave up show business and became a minister for the Nation of Islam's Boston temple in 1956. At first, he was a devoted follower of Malcolm X. He even tried to speak like Malcolm. But when Malcolm split from the Nation of Islam, Louis turned on him. He called Malcolm a traitor. After Malcolm X was assassinated, Louis became the head of the Nation's Harlem mosque. He quickly became the Nation's number one spokesperson.

Malcolm soon announced that he was forming his own religious organization. It would be similar to the Nation of Islam, but its leader would not be worshiped. The new organization was called the Muslim Mosque, Inc.

Many of Malcolm's beliefs changed when he left the Nation of Islam. But his basic message remained the same. He still believed that blacks would only achieve freedom by fighting for it. He believed that the U.S. government was racist and would not give rights to African Americans unless it was forced to do so. He believed that patience was not a virtue for black citizens, who needed freedom now. He believed that blacks who sided with whites in the social struggle should be stopped. And he still believed that African Americans needed to choose their own leaders and take charge of their own social struggle.

It's a Fact!

Malcolm originally wanted all profits from the book about his life to go to the Nation of Islam. When Malcolm left the Nation, he received death threats. He quickly changed his book contract before anything bad could happen to him. The profits were to go to Muslim Mosque, Inc., or, if he died, to his wife, Betty.

IT'S A FACT!

Malcolm X was called the only person in America who could either start a riot or stop one. Malcolm responded to this saying, "I don't know if I could start one. I don't know if I'd want to stop one."

In 1964, Congress passed the Civil Rights Act. Among other things, this act created new laws against racial discrimination and segregation. Even this did not impress Malcolm. He said that the new laws didn't go far enough. He pointed to outbreaks of racial violence in northern cities as evidence of the anger that was building. He believed people would soon explode with rage. Malcolm's critics, both white and black, continued to accuse him of promoting violence.

JOURNEY TO MECCA

Away from Elijah Muhammad's direction, Malcolm was free to think for himself. Malcolm began to think about the black struggle for independence in international terms. Maybe he was thinking about his father's earlier work with Marcus Garvey. Malcolm also became more

interested in exploring traditional Islam. One of
the goals for traditional Muslims is to make a hajj,
or holy journey, to Mecca. This city in Saudi
Arabia is the birthplace of the prophet
Muhammad and the religious capital of Islam.
Black Muslims are not required to make this
journey, but Malcolm decided to do it.

FIVE PILLARS OF ISLAM

Malcolm knew that five pillars, or duties, are required of traditional
Muslims. The first is to worship no one but Allah. The second is to pray
daily. The third duty is to stop or limit eating before sunset for the month
of Ramadan, the holiest Islamic period. The fourth pillar is to give to the
poor. And the fifth is to make a pilgrimage, or religious visit, to Mecca.

**Every year, hundreds of thousands of Muslims journey to the Grand
Mosque in Mecca, Saudi Arabia.**

Malcolm told his sister Ella that he wanted to visit Mecca but that he didn't have enough money to pay for the trip. Ella gave him the money he needed.

Malcolm left for Mecca on April 13, 1964. His wife and children did not go with him. Malcolm felt strangely out of place among the traditional Muslims. He didn't know the prayers or the customs. He didn't speak Arabic, the main language of the region.

In Saudi Arabia, Malcolm met light-skinned men who would have been considered "white" in

Malcolm X during his journey to Mecca, Saudi Arabia

the United States. But these were Muslims and his brothers in the faith. People on their way to Mecca were expected to wear traditional Islamic clothing. This meant a covering of white cloths, with one worn over the shoulder and the other around the waist. This was the way Malcolm dressed during his religious visit. He prayed and slept and ate next to Muslims of all colors.

In his travel journal, Malcolm wrote, "There were tens of thousands of pilgrims, from all over the world. They were of all colors, from blue-eyed blonds to black-skinned Africans. But we were all participating in the same ritual, displaying a spirit of unity and brotherhood that my experiences in America had led me to believe never could exist between the white and the non-white. . . . America needs to understand Islam, because this is the one religion that erases from its society the race problem."

In Mecca, Malcolm prayed at the sacred stone in the Kaaba. The Kaaba is a place of worship first used by the biblical leaders Abraham and Ishmael four thousand years ago. The black stone inside the building is an important symbol of Islam.

While he was in Saudi Arabia, Malcolm wrote an open letter to the press. In his letter, he said,

"[I am] spellbound by the graciousness [kindness] I see displayed all around me by people of all colors. Despite my firm convictions [beliefs], I have always been a man who tries to face facts, and to accept the reality of life as new experience and new knowledge unfolds it."

Following his visit to Mecca, Malcolm X again changed his name. He became El-Hajj Malik El-Shabazz. According to Islam, the Shabazz were a tribe of black people who moved from East Asia to Africa fifty thousand years ago. El Hajj meant that Malcolm had been to Mecca. And Malik is the Arabic version of Malcolm.

WORLD LEADER

AFTER HIS VISIT TO MECCA, Malcolm
was allowed to meet with Prince Faisal, the
ruler of Saudi Arabia. This meeting took place
in April 1964. Faisal said he had heard of the
Black Muslims. From what Faisal had read, he
thought the Black Muslims did not understand
the true nature of Islam. Malcolm explained
that he had separated from the Black Muslims.
By going to Mecca, Malcolm was trying to
understand true Islam for the first time.

(Above)
**Malcolm X
and Saudi
Arabia's
Prince
Faisal
during their
1964
meeting**

Malcolm also visited Nigeria, a West
African nation that has a large Muslim

77

population. He spoke at one of the nation's top colleges, Ibadan University. In his speech, Malcolm discussed his plans to join blacks in America with blacks from the rest of the world. Many leaders had called on black people to "return to Africa." Malcolm explained that this did not have to be done physically. It could be done economically.

Malcolm thought black Americans could start their own businesses with the help of African governments. Black consumers would buy products made only by black people. They would trade only with black-owned businesses. In this way, black people would not have to depend on white people for anything. This idea was called Pan-Africanism. It meant that all Africans would work together, even those who no longer lived in Africa. Malcolm believed that African Americans must become economically independent, as many black Africans were. Otherwise, they would make little progress socially.

Nigerian leaders told Malcolm that they thought black Americans were already making much progress. This was what they heard from white Americans who did business in Nigeria. Malcolm informed the Nigerians that the truth was not so positive.

From Nigeria, Malcolm flew to Accra, Ghana, also in West Africa. He spoke to the lawmakers in Ghana. He received an English version of the Quran, the holy book of Islam.

From Ghana, Malcolm traveled elsewhere in Africa—to Senegal and then to Morocco. Malcolm's last stop on his African tour was Algiers, Algeria. At that time, Algeria was fighting for independence from the French.

On his tour of Africa, Malcolm visited the countries labeled on this map. He also visited neighboring Saudi Arabia.

Malcolm holds his daughter Ilyasah after returning from Mecca.

Malcolm returned to New York on May 21, 1964. He was a changed man. He had gone to Africa to find his true religion. He had learned that many of his earlier beliefs about race were false. White people were not really devils, and black people were not really the chosen ones. He also learned that the rest of the world saw him as a representative of America's black population. This allowed him to do things he had never dreamed of.

NEW DIRECTIONS

Malcolm returned to his family at their home in Queens, a section of New York City. But Malcolm's wife and daughters did not get to see him very often. He was a loving husband and father, but he was also one of the world's busiest men. Betty spent much of her time answering the phone and taking messages for Malcolm. She took care of all family business. Malcolm admitted that he had never bought his daughters a present on his own. Betty always took care of that for him. Even when Malcolm was in New York, he worked eighteen-hour days and came home only to sleep. After Malcolm left the Nation, he supported his family with donations from the members of his mosque.

IT'S A FACT!

Malcolm's fourth daughter, Gamilah Lumumba, was born in 1964. She is named after an African leader named Patrice Lumumba. He'd led the fight to gain independence for Zaire (modern Congo). Political opponents murdered him in 1961, and he became a national hero.

In June 1964, Malcolm formed another new organization. He had just turned thirty-nine years old. Malcolm already had the Muslim Mosque, which was set up as a traditional Islamic temple. But he also needed a nonreligious framework for his work. He called the new group the Organization of Afro-American Unity (OAAU). He hoped it would "include all people of African descent in the Western Hemisphere, as well as our brothers and sisters on the African Continent." The OAAU would work for human rights for all black people, regardless of their differences in location, religion, or job.

Malcolm returned to Africa and the Middle East for eighteen weeks in the summer and fall of 1964. He went as a spokesperson for the OAAU. He traveled without his family again. During this trip, he met with many African leaders. These included President Gamal Abdel Nasser of Egypt, President Nnamdi Azikiwe of Nigeria, and President Julius Nyerere of Tanzania. By October, Malcolm had met with the leaders of eleven African nations. After this trip, Malcolm told his followers, "My dearest friends have come to include . . . Christians, Jews, Buddhists, Hindus, agnostics, and even atheists! [Agnostics are not certain if there is a God. Atheists do not believe in God at all.] . . . My friends today are black, brown, red, yellow, and *white*!"

For years, white people who believed in Malcolm's ideas had been asking him what they could do to help. At one time, Malcolm had said

Malcolm X at a press conference following his return from Africa in November 1964.

there was nothing they could do. But he had changed his mind. He still did not allow white people to join his organization. But he did encourage them to teach other whites about unfair social practices in the United States.

CHAPTER 8

THREATS AND DANGER

FOR YEARS, MALCOLM HAD FELT that he would die a violent death. He wrote, "If I take the kind of things in which I believe, then add to that the kind of temperament [personality] that I have, plus the one hundred percent dedication I have to whatever I believe in—these are ingredients which make it just about impossible for me to die of old age."

Malcolm also knew that he had enemies. He was hated by white racists and by some members of the Nation of Islam. Some Black Muslims had pledged to kill him for "betraying" Elijah Muhammad.

FIREBOMB

On February 14, 1965, an explosion woke Malcolm and his family at 3:00 A.M. Their house in Queens had been firebombed with a handmade explosive device. The scene must have reminded Malcolm of his childhood, when a white mob burned down his family's house.

He screamed instructions in the dark as his house burned. He gathered up his children and made sure everyone got outside safely. The New York City Fire Department needed a full hour to put out the fire. Half of Malcolm's home was destroyed. The family had no insurance to cover their loss. The threats on Malcolm's life were real. His family was in danger too. Malcolm took them to stay at a friend's house.

A few days later, Malcolm was invited to speak in Selma, Alabama. The invitation came from members of a civil rights group called the Student Nonviolent Coordinating Committee. Members of Dr. King's Southern

IT'S A FACT!

Minister James X of the New York mosque accused Malcolm of starting the fire himself to gain publicity. Malcolm was outraged.

Christian Leadership Conference tried to keep Malcolm from coming to Selma. They thought that Malcolm's presence would spark riots. But Malcolm came anyway, and he spoke with his usual passion. He saw the South as a good place to recruit new members to his mosque. He sensed that southern blacks were becoming impatient with the slow pace of progress on civil rights. Their nonviolent protests were not getting results fast enough.

The Last Speech

Back in New York, Malcolm was scheduled to speak at the Audubon Ballroom in Harlem on Sunday afternoon, February 21, 1965. He invited Betty and all four of his daughters to attend the meeting. Betty was then pregnant with their fifth child. After the fire and the death threats, Malcolm had tried to keep his family away from his public activities. But on this day, he asked them to watch him speak.

Four hundred wooden chairs had been set up in the ballroom. Not much security was in place. No one searched guests at the door. That was Malcolm's plan. He didn't want people to feel uncomfortable. He did allow members of his personal security force to be in the room.

Malcolm dressed as he always did. He wore a dark suit, a white shirt, and a slender tie. He sat backstage listening to the speakers before him. He planned his own remarks. Looking out at the room, he could see that three-quarters of the seats were full. On this day, Malcolm didn't plan to talk about the black man's battle against the white man. Instead, he planned to talk about the foolishness of black men fighting other black men.

STRUCK DOWN

After the opening speeches, Malcolm was introduced. He moved to the front of the room and spoke his traditional greeting, "[Peace be with you], brothers and sisters." Before he could begin his speech, however, a noise broke out in the audience. Almost everyone, including Malcolm, looked out into the seats to see what was going on.

"Take your hand out of my pocket!" a man yelled. Malcolm tried to calm the situation down. "Hold it! Hold it! Don't get excited," he said.

As this was going on, a smoke bomb was set off at the back of the ballroom. Someone poured water on the bomb and put out the fire before the room could fill with smoke. A man sitting in the front row stood up. He pulled a shotgun from beneath his coat and fired into Malcolm's chest. Two other men with handguns ran forward and pumped more bullets into Malcolm's body.

Malcolm was struck sixteen times. Most of the shots hit his chest. But one struck his cheek and another hit the middle finger of his left hand. Malcolm's hand went to his chest when the firing started. Then his other arm flew up. As he fell over backward on the stage, his head hit a stagehand, and he knocked over two chairs.

The Audubon Ballroom in Harlem, New York, after Malcolm's murder

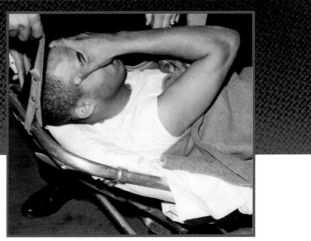

Talmadge Hayer was a suspect in Malcolm X's killing. Here he covers his face as he is taken on a stretcher to a nearby hospital.

The ballroom exploded with activity. Betty ran onto the stage screaming. The shooters scattered in different directions. No two witnesses seemed to have seen the same thing.

An armed member of Malcolm's security force chased one of the shooters from the ballroom. This shooter was later identified as Talmadge Hayer. The security guard shot Hayer in the leg. Hayer made it to the sidewalk, dragging his wounded leg. But angry spectators began to kick him. The crowd might have killed him, if police hadn't come to his rescue.

The police officers who were supposed to be stationed at the ballroom for Malcolm's appearance were nowhere to be seen. But two officers riding by in a patrol car had seen the angry mob kicking the fleeing shooter. The police fired two warning shots into the air to break up the attack.

Malcolm was taken to the hospital, where he was pronounced dead on the operating table at 3:15 P.M. The next day, Elijah Muhammad spoke about Malcolm's death, saying "Malcolm died according to his preaching. He seems to have taken weapons as his god. Therefore, we couldn't tolerate a man like that. He preached war. We preach peace."

More violence followed. On February 22, the Black Muslim mosque in Harlem was firebombed. The bomb caused a huge blaze. During the fire, a wall collapsed and two fire engines parked at the curb were smashed. Five firefighters were injured fighting the blaze.

MALCOLM'S FUNERAL

Meanwhile, Betty was struggling with the reality of her loss. She found it hard to find a location for Malcolm's funeral. Everyone was afraid violence would erupt. But Bishop Alvin Childs agreed to hold the funeral at Harlem's Faith Temple. The temple was a former movie theater that could hold fourteen hundred people.

After Malcolm's death, his body was put into a glass-covered coffin. Then it was displayed for public viewing at the Unity Funeral Home in Harlem. Twenty-two thousand people came to see him.

After the viewing, Sheik Ahmed Hassoun, Malcolm's spiritual adviser, prepared his body for burial according to Islamic traditions. Sheik Hassoun bathed Malcolm's body in holy oils and

People pay their respects to Malcolm X at the Unity Funeral Home. The glass that covered Malcolm's coffin during public viewing was removed for photos.

draped it in seven white burial cloths, so that only Malcolm's face could be seen.

Faith Temple wasn't nearly big enough for the crowd that wanted to attend Malcolm's funeral. Seventeen hundred mourners packed into the building. More than six thousand people lined the streets outside.

Actor Ossie Davis delivered the funeral speech. He said, "Many will ask what Harlem finds to honor in this stormy, controversial and bold young captain—and we will smile. . . . They will say that he is of hate—a fanatic, a racist—who can only bring evil to the cause for which you struggle.

"And we will answer and say unto them: Did you ever talk to Brother Malcolm? Did you ever touch him, or have him smile at you? Did you ever really listen to him? Did he ever do a mean thing? Was he ever himself associated with violence or any public disturbance? For if you did you would know him. And if you knew him you would know why we must honor him: Malcolm was our manhood, our living, black manhood! This was his meaning to his people. And, in honoring him, we honor the best in ourselves." Malcolm was buried at the Ferncliff Cemetery in Hartsdale, New York.

Betty Shabazz (center), pregnant with twins, mourns at the grave of Malcolm X.

Not long afterward, people in Harlem learned that Malcolm had died without any money. Betty and the girls were left with no savings, no insurance, and no income. So a fund was set up to help the family.

UNANSWERED QUESTIONS

Within two weeks of the assassination, two more men besides Talmadge Hayer were arrested for the shooting. They were Norman 3X Butler and

Norman 3X Butler *(left)* and Thomas 15X Johnson *(center, right)* at the police station after their arrests

Thomas 15X Johnson. Both were members of the Nation of Islam.

After Malcolm's death, Betty publicly accused Louis Farrakhan of having a role in the assassination. Two months before Malcolm's murder, Farrakhan had written that Malcolm was a "traitor" and that "such a man is worthy of death."

Nevertheless, the New York police claimed to have fully solved the crime of Malcolm's assassination. But doubts surfaced. Early reports said that at least five men were involved in the shooting. Three men had fired weapons. Two others had helped by drawing attention to the back of the ballroom. After the police had arrested the three shooters, they stopped looking for other participants.

Talmadge Hayer confessed to shooting Malcolm. But he always insisted that Johnson and Butler had nothing to do with the assassination. Many were puzzled that Malcolm's security guards didn't notice Johnson and Butler entering the ballroom. They were followers of Elijah Muhammad, not complete strangers. Hayer was not a Muslim. And he said that the Black Muslims did not pay him to murder Malcolm. He admitted that he had committed the crime for money. But he never said who had paid him or who his helpers were.

9 MALCOLM'S MESSAGE

SHORTLY AFTER MALCOLM X'S death, his autobiography was published. This was the life story he had written with journalist Alex Haley.

Time magazine called *The Autobiography of Malcolm X* one of the ten most important nonfiction (factual) books of the twentieth century.

Malcolm's message of black pride and self-reliance lived on after his death. The message inspired political movements, such as the Black Power movement and the Black Panther

IT'S A FACT!

Malcolm and Haley met when Haley interviewed Malcolm for *Playboy* magazine. They worked on Malcolm's autobiography for two years. At first, Malcolm was suspicious of Haley. Eventually, he came to trust the non-Muslim author.

Party. People who fought for black power believed that black people should not try to fit in with white society. Instead, they thought blacks should create a social and economic system outside the white system.

The Black Power movement considered Malcolm its hero. The Black Panther Party was organized in 1966. It fought for full employment and decent housing for black people. The party sought an end to police brutality against blacks. It supported the teaching of black history. Black Panther members wore black leather jackets and carried guns as they patrolled the streets of black neighborhoods.

Black Panther Party members march in New York City in the late 1960s.

After Malcolm's death, Betty gave birth to twin girls, Malikah and Malaak. Betty raised their six girls in a city just north of New York City called Mount Vernon. In 1975, Betty earned her doctorate degree in education at the University of Massachusetts. She became an administrator at Medgar Evans College in Brooklyn.

IT'S A FACT!

The twins born after Malcolm's murder were named Malaak and Malikah. Their names come from Malik, the Arabic form of Malcolm.

Betty Shabazz, pictured here in the early 1990s, earned her doctorate degree in 1975.

In 1985, convicted assassin Norman 3X Butler was released from prison and put on parole. He had served nineteen years for his crime. While in prison, he had changed his name to Muhammad Abdul Aziz.

Memories and Endings

Almost thirty years after Malcolm's death, the feud between his family and the Nation of Islam became headlines again. In 1994, Malcolm and Betty's daughter Qubilah was arrested. She was charged with plotting to hire someone to kill Louis Farrakhan. The charges

Qubilah leaves the courthouse in Minneapolis, Minnesota, after her first hearing. She was accused of hiring someone to kill Louis Farrakhan.

were dropped because there wasn't enough evidence. Later, Betty and Farrakhan ended the feud.

On June 1, 1997, Betty was badly burned in a fire at her apartment in Yonkers, a suburb of New York City. Her twelve-year-old grandson, who was named after Malcolm X, set the fire. The boy was unhappy living with his grandmother and wanted to return to his mother, Qubilah, in Texas.

Over the next three weeks, Betty had five operations to replace her burned skin with artificial skin. But people with such severe burn injuries rarely survive. Betty passed away on June 23, 1997. She was buried beside Malcolm at the Ferncliff Cemetery in Hartsdale.

In March 1998, the Nation of Islam named Muhammad Abdul Aziz to head the temple in Harlem. This meant that one of the men convicted of killing Malcolm was preaching in the same place Malcolm had preached in the 1950s.

The Nation of Islam hired a lie detector expert to interview Aziz about the assassination. Aziz was questioned for three days. Afterward, the expert announced that Aziz was telling the truth when he said he had had nothing to do with

Muhammad Abdul Aziz *(center)* is introduced as the new head of the Nation of Islam's Harlem temple.

Malcolm X's death. Aziz still claims to be innocent in Malcolm's death.

LOOKING FOR ANSWERS

In April 2000, Malcolm's eldest daughter Attallah Shabazz met face-to-face with Louis Farrakhan. Their meeting was arranged by the makers of *60 Minutes*, a TV news program. This was the first-ever meeting between Farrakhan and a member of Malcolm's family. Attallah had been just six years old when she saw her father murdered.

Mike Wallace *(right)* interviews Louis Farrakhan *(left)* and Attallah Shabazz *(center)* for the May 14, 2000, broadcast of *60 Minutes.*

During the program, Farrakhan denied that he had directly ordered Malcolm's assassination. However, he did admit that some of his words might have been misunderstood. Some people might have thought he meant it was all right to kill Malcolm. He accepted partial blame for the killing. Farrakhan explained, "As I may have been [partially at fault] in words that I spoke. . . . I acknowledge that and regret that any word that I have said caused the loss of life of a human being."

A MODERN HERO

Malcolm X has not been forgotten. He remains a hero for black people and for anyone who believes in racial justice and ethnic pride. Many books have been written about Malcolm's life and message. Several cities in the United States have yearly Malcolm X festivals in May to celebrate Malcolm's birthday. He is praised in the lyrics of songs, and his speeches are available on CD.

A man browses through the many Malcolm X titles in his local bookstore.

May 19, 2000, would have been Malcolm's seventy-fifth birthday. On that day, more than seven hundred admirers gathered in the pouring rain at his graveside in Hartsdale, New York. Michael X, a Bronx community leader, said, "I'm glad we didn't bury Malcolm's legacy [history] along with him. And all these people coming

THE MOVIE *MALCOLM X*

In 1992, filmmaker Spike Lee made a major motion picture about Malcolm X. Louis Farrakhan demanded that Lee never mention him in the movie. Denzel Washington starred in the title role. The movie helped create new interest in Malcolm's message.

Denzel Washington (left) played the lead in Spike Lee's *Malcolm X*.

here today shows how much he truly means to our community. His clarity [clearness] of thought, integrity [honesty], vision, courage and, most of all, his humility [humble nature] separated him from the pack when he was alive and even more so today."

Black Panther Party: a political organization founded in California in 1966 by Huey P. Newton and Bobby Seale. The party stressed equality, freedom, and justice for all African Americans and disagreed with the nonviolent strategies of the civil rights movement.

black power: a point of view that formed in the 1960s to push for African Americans to create their own political, economic, and cultural systems

civil rights movement: a group that joined together to push for freedom and equal treatment of African Americans under the law

Harlem: a mostly black residential area of the borough (section) of Manhattan in New York City

hustling: aggressively selling or getting something through dishonest means

integration: the act of bringing together and treating as equals members of different races, such as blacks and whites during the civil rights movement of the mid-1900s

Islam: a major world religion that began in the Middle East more than 1,400 years ago. Followers of Islam are called Muslims. Muslims believe in Allah (God) and in Muhammad as his prophet. The religion's holy book is the Quran.

Ku Klux Klan: a group of people who believe the white race is superior to all other races and have used violence to support their beliefs

Nation of Islam: a modern religion founded in 1930 by Wallace D. Fard based on the traditional religion of Islam. Like Islam, followers of the Nation of Islam (called Black Muslims) worship Allah as the one true God. Unlike traditional Islam, however, Black Muslims believe that white people are evil and that black people are Allah's favorite.

Organization of Afro-American Unity (OAAU): a group formed by Malcolm X in 1964 to work for human rights for all black people, not just Muslims

Pan-Africanism: belief in the unity of all Africans and the end of white rule in Africa

racial discrimination: opinions and actions carried out unfairly against a racial group. Racial discrimination can lead to racial segregation, or the practice of keeping ethnic groups apart.

the South: in the United States, the states that fought against the Union (or North) in the Civil War (1861–1865)

Uncle Tom: a black person who behaves like a servant in front of white people. The term comes from the novel *Uncle Tom's Cabin* by Harriet Beecher Stowe. In the novel, written in 1852, Uncle Tom is a faithful black slave.

Universal Negro Improvement Association (UNIA): an organization that promoted black pride and an independent black Africa, or a place where all African Americans could live without whites. The organization was founded by Marcus Garvey in Jamaica in 1914 and was brought to the United States in 1918.

12 Malcolm X, *The Autobiography of Malcolm X*, with Alex Haley (New York: Ballantine Books, 1964), 11.

13 Ibid., 6.

16–17 Ibid., 37–38.

17 Ibid., 41–42.

19 Walter Dean Myers, *Malcolm X: By Any Means Necessary* (New York: Scholastic Press, 1993), 43.

21 Malcolm X, with Alex Haley, 61.

26 *Malcolm X: A Search for Identity*, VHS, (New York: A&E Home Video: New Video Group, 1995).

26 Jack Rummel, *Malcolm X: Militant Black Leader* (Los Angeles: Melrose Square, 1988), 39.

33 *Malcolm X: A Search for Identity*.

42 Alex Haley, "The Playboy Interview with Malcolm X," *Playboy*, May 1963.

51 "Malcolm X," *Microsoft Encarta Online Encyclopedia 2001*, 1997, Microsoft Corp. http://encarta.msn.htm (May 18, 2001).

56 George Breitman, Herman Porter, and Baxter Smith, *The Assassination of Malcolm X* (New York: Pathfinder Press, 1991), 22.

58 Ibid., 38.

60 Haley.

61 Ibid.

61–63 Ibid.

66 Malcolm X, with Alex Haley, 329.

66 Malcolm X, with Alex Haley, 311–312.

72 Ibid., 403.

75 Ibid., 414.

76 Rummel, 165.

82 Myers, 158.

82 Malcolm X, with Alex Haley, 410.

84 Ibid., 414.

87 Rummel, 175.

87 Malcolm X, with Alex Haley, 473.

87 David Shirley, *Malcolm X: Minister of Justice* (Philadelphia: Chelsea House Publishers, 1994), 28.

90 Malcolm X, with Alex Haley, 479.

92 Ibid., 494.

94 "Farrakhan: I Had Malcolm X Slay Role," *Daily News*, May 11, 2000, 40.

102 William Neuman, "Malcolm X's Daughter Talks with Farrakhan," *New York Post*, May 9, 2000, 40.

104–105 Jack Baxter, "Followers Flock to Malcolm X's Grave on His 75th Birthday," *New York Post*, May 20, 2000, 18.

SELECTED BIBLIOGRAPHY

Baxter, Jack. "Followers Flock to Malcolm X's Grave on His 75th Birthday." *New York Post*, May 20, 2000.

Breitman, George, Herman Porter, and Baxter Smith. *The Assassination of Malcolm X*. New York: Pathfinder Press, 1991.

"Farrakhan: I Had Malcolm X Slay Role." *Daily News*, May 11, 2000.

Goldman, Peter. *The Death and Life of Malcolm X*. New York: Harper and Row, 1973.

Halasa, Malu. *Elijah Muhammad: Religious Leader*. New York: Chelsea House, 1990.

Malcolm X. *The Autobiography of Malcolm X*. With Alex Haley. New York: Ballantine Books, 1964.

Malcolm X: A Search for Identity. VHS. A&E Biography. New York: A&E Home Video: New Video Group, 1995.

Patterson, Charles. *The Civil Rights Movement*. New York: Facts on File, 1995.

Ross, Barbara. "Guilty Plea in Theft of Malcolm X Diary." *Daily News*, July 18, 2000.

Rummel, Jack. *Malcolm X: Militant Black Leader*. Los Angeles: Melrose Square, 1988.

Shirley, David. *Malcolm X: Minister of Justice*. Philadelphia: Chelsea House Publishers, 1994.

FURTHER READING AND WEBSITES

Adoff, Arnold. *Malcolm X*. New York: HarperCollins, 2000.

Crushshon. Theresa. *Malcolm X*. Chanhassen, MN: Child's World, 2001.

Darby, Jean. *Martin Luther King Jr.* Minneapolis: Lerner Publications Company, 2005.

Donovan, Sandra. *Marcus Garvey.* Chicago: Raintree, 2003.

Downing, David. *Malcolm X.* Crystal Lake, IL: Heinemann Library, 2003.

Draper, Allison Stark. *The Assassination of Malcolm X.* New York: Rosen Publishing Group, 2001.

Graves, Renee. *Malcolm X.* Danbury, CT: Children's Press, 2003.

Jeffrey, Laura S. *Betty Shabazz: Sharing the Vision of Malcolm X.* Berkeley Heights, NJ: Enslow Publishers, 2000.

Malcolm X and Alex Haley. *The Autobiography of Malcolm X.* New York: Ballantine Books, 1964.

The Malcolm X Museum
http://www.the malcolmxmuseum.org
Under construction in Harlem, the Malcolm X Museum will house memorabilia (things that belonged to Malcolm), as well as photos, audio versions of speeches, and more. The website gives updates on the status of the construction and other community news.

The Official Malcolm X Site
http://www.cmgww.com/historic/malcolm
The official site has photos, a biography, a timeline, speeches, and much more that celebrates the life of Malcolm X.

Sagan, Miriam. *Malcolm X.* San Diego, CA: Lucent Books, 1997.

Schraff, Anne E. *Marcus Garvey: Controversial Champion of Black Pride.* Berkeley Heights, NJ: Enslow Publishers, 2004.

Schulman, Arlene. *Muhammad Ali.* Minneapolis: Lerner Publications Company, 2005.

Wormser, Richard. *American Islam: Growing Up Muslim in America.* New York: Walker & Co., 2002.

PHOTO ACKNOWLEDGMENTS

Photographs are used with the permission of: © Bettmann/CORBIS, pp. 5, 8, 11, 25, 32, 34, 36, 44, 52, 62, 80, 83, 84, 89, 93, 94 (left), 94 (right), 97; National Archives, p. 10 [306-NT-650-1]; © Bureau L.A. Collection/CORBIS, p. 20; © AP/Wide World Photos, pp. 29, 57, 68, 69, 88, 91, 99, 101; © Getty Images, pp. 40, 54, 74, 77; Schomburg Center for Research in Black Culture, p. 49; © Time Life Pictures/Getty Images, p. 50; © CORBIS, p. 59; The John F. Kennedy Library, p. 65; © SUHAIB SALEM/Reuters/CORBIS, p. 73; Bill Hauser, p. 79; © JONES JULIA/CORBIS SYGMA, p. 98; © CBS/Landov, p. 102; © Jacques M. Chenet/CORBIS, p. 103; © Photofest, p. 104.

Cover: © Bettmann/CORBIS.